How to Invest in Real Estate Successfully

50 secret tips from the wealthiest Real Estate investors in the world

Mandeep Bhalla

Follow On Instagram
@Realestate.mentor

Copyright © 2019 by The Bhalla Real Estate Group

All rights reserved. No part of this publication may be reproduced, distributed, or transmitted in any form or by any means, including photocopying, recording, or other electronic or mechanical methods, without the prior written permission of the publisher, except in the case or brief quotations embodied in critical reviews and certain other noncommercial uses permitted by copyright law. For permission requests, write to the publisher, addressed "Attention: Permissions Coordinator," at the address below.

34146 Cedar Ave
Abbotsford, BC, V2S2W1
Mandeepbhalla88@gmail.com

Table Of Contents

1. Believe In The Market — 9
2. Never Sell Investment Real Estate Trade It — 12
3. Opportunities Always Exist — 14
4. Choose Your Realtor Wisely — 16
5. You Make The Most Money On The Day You Buy — 18
6. Go Where The Money Is — 21
7. Look For Pre-Foreclosure Deals — 23
8. Look for Strong Anchor Stores — 27
9. Diversify Your Investments — 29
10. Find The Right Partners — 31
11. Develop In An Area Where Growth is Coming — 33
12. Use the 10 Percent Rule — 35
13. Time The Market — 37
14. Maintain Your Objectivity — 39
15. Usually The First Offer Is The Best Offer — 42
16. Begin With The End In Mind — 44
17. Negotiate An Amazing Deal — 47
18. Real Estate Will Always Appreciate in Value — 49

19. Who's On Your Advisory Team	50
20. Land Is A Monopoly	52
21. Financial Literacy Is Key	54
22. Buy Real Estate Now	59
23. Rezone Your Property & Increase the Value	60
24. Don't Do This	62
25. Buy Low, Sell High	63
26. Use Leverage Wisely	64
27. Strategise	66
28. Lenders Know Best	68
29. A Taxing Issue	70
30. Cash Flow Is King	73
31. Protect your real estate investment, screen your tenants	75
32. When It's Hard To Find A Good Deal As A Buyer It's A Great Time To Sell	77
33. Never Lose Money	79
34. Lucky Or Smart	80
35. Keep An Eye On Your Investments	83
36. Never Stop Learning	85
37. Disclose	87

38. Location, Location, Location	88
39. Construct your own investment	91
40. Create Cash Flow	94
41. NOI, GRM, CAP Rate	96
42. Risk and Reward	99
43. The 3 Kings	103
44. Don't Over Renovate	105
45. Numbers Never Lie	109
46. Create a Rainy Day Fund	110
47. Don't Chase the Market	112
48. Find a Mentor	114
49. Think Big	116
50. Take Control of Your Future	118

Introduction

This book is a compilation of the best real estate advice I have come across while reading real estate investing books. These tips offer a lot of insight from super wealthy real estate investors.

Real Estate is not rocket science. Real estate investing is simple, however it is not easy to execute. There are proven strategies that can be understood and put into action. If you model the most successful real estate investors, you will achieve your real estate goals. The main goal of real estate investing is to create generational wealth.

You have to approach real estate investing the same way you would your job or your business. There is no such thing as passive real estate investing. You have to be very involved in every step of the way. This book is great for laying the foundation of successful real estate investing. I share the advice from the best real estate investors in the world. I have learned so much from these people. You always learn from your mistakes, but it is way cheaper to learn from other people's experiences and mistakes. If you can find a mentor, that is one of the major keys to success

This book is great for beginner investors and seasoned experts as well. If you want to become a millionaire, real estate is the perfect vehicle to do so. 90% of millionaires have used real estate to amass a significant portion of their wealth. You can do the same as well

1. Believe In The Market

"Throughout time real estate has endured as one of the most effective if not the most effective vehicles for creating wealth and security over the long run."

Harvey E. Green

Since the beginning of time people have needed a roof over their head. When you combine a need such as shelter with massive tax advantages, lower volatility and amazing appreciating over time, you get an amazing investment product. Real estate investments are tangible assets that will be here 1000s of years from now. If you are the owner of commercial properties, someone will be paying you rent, and rent always increases over time..

The business that operates in your commercial unit will be long gone, but the building itself and especially the land will still be there. The Land will also be worth a lot more money than what you bought it for. If you believe in the real estate market, it can create billions in wealth for you. Many, many people take advantage of real estate to get rich.

The top five land owners in the US at the time of research are:

1. John Malone, former CEO of Tele-Communications Inc: 2.2m acres
2. Ted Turner, founder of CNN: 2m acres
3. Stan Kroenke, owner of LA Rams: 1.38m acres
4. Peter Buck, co-founder of Subway: 925k acres
5. Jeff Bezos, founder of Amazon: 420k acres

These people created massive wealth in their respective businesses, and then they invested that wealth in purchasing land. These billionaires have created generational wealth. This wealth will be passed on to their heirs. These billionaires understand that land retains value over the long run.

However, if you are new to real estate investing, I would recommend cash flowing properties instead. I will discuss in further detail later in the book.

2. Never Sell Investment Real Estate Trade It

"If you have real estate investments in the US, take advantage of a 1031 exchange, which allows you to trade like kind investment properties with limited or no tax consequences. Don't Sell."

Jim Gillespie

One of the biggest regrets that most real estate investors have is that they sold a lot of their properties. The goal is to have real estate pay you, forever! Once you sell the investment, the stream of income is gone. If you do need the money, trade the property. Use the 1031 exchange and upgrade for a better property with more cash flow.

Basically, you are allowed to defer paying property capital gains tax when you sell real estate. You sell the property, you do not pay tax (at the moment) and you are able to use that money to purchase a new real estate investment. You have 45 days to identify a new property that you wish to purchase and 180 days to close on that property.

The replacement property has to be "like kind", which means that replacement property must be the same in character. For example exchanging a fourplex for a multifamily would be allowed. The value has to be equal to or greater than your current value.

Deferring taxes has massive benefits. A dollar saved today to purchase more real estate is worth much more than paying your capital gains tax.

3. Opportunities Always Exist

"Never a wrong time to purchase real estate. The only constant is change. It brings new and different opportunities. Choose the right strategy."

Dorothy Herman

I have learned that success in real estate is not random. There is no need to reinvent the wheel. Take some time to know the statistics of the market you plan to invest in. If you know your market, then you can definitely find deals. Since real estate has been bought and sold, people have always found opportunities to make money.

Many people fear recessions and depressions in the economy, however the most astute investors view these times very differently. If you are a real estate investor you must change the way you think about a downturn in the economy. From my perspective, a slow down in the housing market means that real estate is now on sale. This is a great time to be purchasing investments.

You must deploy different strategies for different times in the market cycle. For example, after the housing market crash many home builders went out of business because no one was buying new homes. However, the renovation market was booming. The renovation market is known to make big gains when the market is flat.

4. Choose Your Realtor Wisely

"I'm a big believer in a high quality realtor and I endorse realtors for that reason."

Dave Ramsey

There is a big difference in hiring a realtor to sell your home and hiring a realtor to purchase a big real estate investment. You do not want to hire a Joe blow realtor to purchase an investment property.

Look for a realtor that has market knowledge, negotiating power, exclusive listings, and check previous sales history.

A great realtor has access to information and listings that the public does not. Furthermore, he/she uses their skills and experience to get you a great deal. Majority of the time these pro realtors have created dream teams consisting of lawyers, notaries, building inspectors, accountants and management companies. Get the realtor to introduce you to their dream team.

If you plan on being a super wealthy real estate investor, building a relationship with an expert investment realtor is a major key.

5. You Make The Most Money On The Day You Buy

"You will make the most money because of your due diligence, your astute assessment and your guts to act."

Ozzie Jurock

To make the most money on the day you buy, you must:

1. Purchase in a buyers market.

If you purchase in a buyers market, you have much more negotiating power than if you have to outbid 10 other offers. In a buyers market there is a huge amount of inventory to choose from. Usually sellers have been sitting on the market for a fairly long time and almost become desperate to sell.

2. Search for the deals where the seller is very motivated to get rid of property.

This can be a divorce situation. People are very motivated to sell in divorces and will let the property go for a much lower price than the fair market value. If the current owner of a property is unable to make their mortgage payments, eventually the bank will foreclose on the property. Find pre-foreclosures and make them an offer. The owner of a home never wants to end up being foreclosed upon. It is a very stressful situation to be in when the bank forecloses on your home, and these types of sellers are VERY motivated to sell.

3.   *Buy a value add property where you can renovate and increase rents.*

Always buy something where you can increase the value. Many of the greatest real estate investors know this secret. Hate him or love him, Donald Trump is a prime example of someone who buys distressed real estate and then transforms it.

Donald Trump is a real estate investor who takes this rule very seriously. A prime example is when Donald bought the Hotel Commodore on 42 street in Manhattan. Hotel Commodore was once revered as one of the best hotels in New York, however over time the hotel became less successful and actually lost $1.5 million dollars in the last year of operation.

Eventually it became an eye sore. This is when Donald Trump stepped in. He purchased the hotel, did a renovation of $100 million dollars and reopened the hotel as the Grand Hyatt.

Recently The Grand Hyatt bought out Donal Trump's share for the price of $130 million dollars. Now that is adding value and flipping.

6. Go Where The Money Is

"Play in the premium markets. Go to the top end of the market. Premium properties even at current market rates will seem cheap in a couple of years."

Phil Ruffin

There will always be someone in the world that has more than enough money to purchase a premium piece of property. The money is in the premium real estate markets. Markets like New York, Vancouver, LA are premium markets. If you purchased an investment in one of those cities 10 or 15 years ago, you would now have a lot of equity built up. You would be profitable irregardless of the market condition.

The premium markets are usually the first to get hit when there is a recession and they are also the first ones to bounce back as well. This is because people will always see value in purchasing in a great city or neighbourhood. Why not purchase the premium piece of land at a discount.

7. Look For Pre-Foreclosure Deals

"By the time a home has gone into foreclosure it's too late. There is already a plethora of investors eyeing the deal. They will bid the deal up. Look for pre foreclosure deals."
M. Anthony Carr

Savvy investors will never overpay for a deal because they do not get emotional about the property. Don't get caught up in the fact that the subject property is a foreclosure and must be a discounted deal. Know the maximum price you would pay for the property before going to court or an auction.

Canadian banks never allow a property to be sold for less than 20% of the fair market value. The US market is a little different and definitely provides bigger opportunities. Get in touch with a realtor who is proficient in foreclosure home sales.

If you cannot find a pre-foreclosure, find a foreclosure.

This is a quick overview of how the court system works in Canada:

1. View property and Submit an offer.(If there is an accepted offer already, then wait for court date).

2. Get an accepted offer. Conduct your due diligence. Give your deposit. Still have to go to court. Where other people can bid on the property.

3. Once there is an accepted offer in place, the bank requests a court date to approve the sale. Setting a court date takes about 2 to four weeks.

While waiting for the court date, interested buyers can still view the property and can also find out your accepted offer price.

If another buyer likes the property and is willing to pay more than your accepted offer, they can come to court on the scheduled court date and submit an offer.

If no one shows up at court and you have the only offer, then judge will approve your sale.

5.	When you are in court you will be able to give one last offer. You will submit in a sealed envelope your offer to the judge. The other parties will also be submitting their offers. The other parties cannot include any subjects in their offers.

6.	The judge will open all the offers. He/She will decide which party has the best offer by considering the following; price, completion, deposit and will decide who has the best offer and then approve the sale to the buyer.

A great realtor will be able to guide you through this process. Purchasing a foreclosure or pre-foreclosure is a great way of building instant equity. That basically means that you purchased a home for below market value.

8. Look for Strong Anchor Stores

"When investing, look for strong anchor stores. Stores like Walmart and Starbucks spend millions of dollars doing research to locate prime property so their stores will be profitable."

One of the biggest keys to success in real estate is to buy real estate investments near strong anchor stores. When looking for potential investments, make sure your investment has a great walk score. I would prefer to invest close to Whole Foods, Walmart, Costco, Starbucks, Universities, and elementary Schools. The opposite is also true. If Walmart just shut down a store location, that is a great indication NOT to invest in that area.

Younger families are considering the location of their home more now than ever before. Young families and millenials want to live in a home that has a high walk score. A high walk score means that you can easily walk to shopping, restaurants and other points of interest.

Grant Cardone, who is a very successful and famous real estate investor in the US, heavily considers what is in the vicinity of his potential real estate purchase. I have seen many of his interviews where he speaks about how he loves when there is a Starbucks and Whole Foods across the street from his investment. People who are shopping at Whole Foods and Starbucks have disposable income. They are great middle class citizens that drive the local economy. They are able to pay their rent on time. They will be the driving force behind the appreciation of your real estate investment.

9. Diversify Your Investments

"It's commonly preached that the best real estate investment is the one in your backyard. While there is a merit to understand the area in which you are investing. I believe you're limiting your profitability potential by only considering a small geographic area. By considering investments in other countries you'll have a large pool of investments and ultimately better opportunities. Investing across a large geographical area also further diversifies your investments and protects your portfolio against the volatility of local markets."

Unknown

The US market is full of opportunities the rest of the world only dreams of. It is a little complicated investing across borders, but I think it is definitely worth it. If you can find a foreign opportunity, take advantage of it. You will have to get in touch with lawyers and accountants from your home country and the country you plan to invest in as well. Lawyers and accountants are key in setting up a successful structure for your company if you want to be tax efficient.

If you live in Canada and want to invest in the US, you are definitely not the first person to have this idea. I would contact a cross border CPA and lawyer to get started. There is also a ton of podcasts that talk about this topic.

RBC has a sister bank in the US. They would be able to finance your deal. They do however require a 40% down on your first deal. They may also be able to point you in the right direction when it comes to creating contacts in the States.

10. Find The Right Partners

"The right choice of partners will not only improve the likelihood of strong financial rewards but also makes life easier when things don't go as planned."
                                              Thomas E. Dobrowski

Look for like minded partners. Make sure you have the same long term and short term goals for the property. If you disagree on the direction of the business plan, it can be very detrimental to the relationship. It is important to discuss all aspects of the venture. You need to discuss; the roles, where capital will be coming from, how are profits going to be distributed, and most importantly how is the work going to be split up?

I have had a lot of success meeting people with meetup.com. You can find a lot of like minded people at these networking events. There is a strong possibility that you will be rubbing shoulders with big investors that have large portfolios. Networking for partners is definitely something you will have to learn to enjoy. Get out of your comfort zone and go to a local meetup.

11. Develop In An Area Where Growth is Coming

"If you're a little early or a little wrong the market will bail you out. If you develop in an area where growth has been and growth is not continuing, when you are wrong, you are wrong forever."

Robert Boykin

The million dollar question is, how can you predict where the growth is going? Look for migration reports on cities. After reading migration reports, you will know what the net migration for the city is. This means, you will know if more people are leaving or coming to a city. Also, find out where the jobs are going. New jobs are a great way of determining what the house prices of the area will be in the coming years. While doing research in the beginning of 2020 i can tell you that people are leaving cities with these characteristics;

1. Affordable
2. High traffic and congestion
3. High crime rates
4. High unemployment rate

For the US, this website allows you to do some research on net migration: netmigration.wisc.edu.

For Canada:
https://www.statcan.gc.ca/eng/start

12. Use the 10 Percent Rule

"The annual gross rent must be at least 10 percent of the purchase price."

Don R. Campbell

This is a great rule to filter properties. There are millions of potential investment properties on the market at any given time. You do not want to waste time analyzing all of them. The 10% percent rule is a quick way of determining which properties are worth further investigation.

It is a very simple formula to screen investment opportunities. The annual gross rent must be at least 10 percent of the purchase price.

Example:

*Monthly rent x 12 = Gross Annual Rent

***Purchase price x 10% = must equal Gross Annual Rent

Property purchase price is $175,000. Property can be rented for $1,500 a month.

*$1,500 x 12 = $18,000
***$175,000 x 10% = 17,500

The gross rent is $500 more than the threshold. The threshold being 10% of the purchase price.

As you can see with the calculation above, this is a property worth further analysis. This is just one calculation that can be used to analyse a property. Basically what an investor is looking for when doing this calculation is cash flow. You want to be able to pay your mortgage, expenses and still be left with positive cash flow. In Real estate positive cash flow trumps everything.

13. Time The Market

"The cycle will create excess and shortages, know where the real estate market is before making a big decision like purchasing or selling your property. "

Mandeep Bhalla

Buyers markets are great for finding deals and negotiating your terms. Seller's market are great for selling your properties and making huge profits.

If you want to learn how to time the market and make a killing in real estate investing, there is a great book written solely on the real estate cycle. This book is "The Secret Life of Real Estate and Banking" written by Phillip J Anderson. In this book, Phillips analyzes data going back hundreds of years and presents the leading indicators that you can use to identify where the market is headed. It would be hard to summarize here but there is a lot written on the subject.

The real estate cycle has been very prominent throughout history and it continues to repeat itself. Buy Low and sell high. You will make a ton of money and you will also look like a genius to people who are oblivious of this cycle.

14. Maintain Your Objectivity

"Do all the analysis and if it does not generate the economic returns you require, pass on it. Never look back, not just in real estate but in life in general. A deal is never as good as it seems or as bad as it seems."

Jorge Perez

This is very straight forward advice, don't let emotions cloud your judgement. If the investment meets your requirements in terms of return on investment, pull the trigger, if not, move on.

You will come across a lot deals. To make life easier, write down your requirements for your ideal investment. For example; you want your investment to give you a return of 6%, your budget is $500,000, you want a multifamily with no less than 16 units. With clearly defined requirements it will be much easier to screen deals.

When you have strict requirements, you will not dwell on investments that you possibly missed. Never fall in love with the deal, maintain your objectivity.

Below are 10 questions that Grant Cardone always asks the selling realtor or the owner before he purchases an investment.

1. When did the seller purchase this investment?
2. How much did they purchase this for?
3. How would you rate this location?
4. Which financials can we rely on to purchase?
5. What is the debt underwriting?
6. What do you like most about this deal?
7. What do you like least about this investment?
8. What else do you have that is listed or off market that is similar to this?
9. Other than price what terms will motivate the seller?
10. In your mind who is the ideal buyer?

11. How much interest have you had on this investment?
12. What would be the future exit? How do I sell this in the future?

I believe these questions will help you in creating a business plan and goals for your investment.

15. Usually The First Offer Is The Best Offer

"Many sellers believe if an offer is received easily there is an ocean and buyers who will pay a higher price. An offer received on the first days of the property being on the market is more valuable than any other offer that will be made. The next offer may not come until a price reduction is done. You have achieved your first goal of finding an interested buyer, now sell the property."

Richard Courtney

You can ask any real estate agent about this one, and they will agree! This is because the most active buyers are usually searching the market vigorously for a deal or home to live in. They are also very informed on what a good and bad deal is, because they have seen the inventory of homes and investment properties. So when they make an offer on your property, it is a great marker of what the value of your property is. Also remember, your home is only worth what someone will pay for it.

The best investors in the world know that real estate investing comes down to numbers. Many investors pass on great offers when they are selling their investment property. These investors convince themselves that there is a huge pool of buyers that will fall in love with their property and continue to offer higher properties.

The future is never guaranteed, when you get a great offer, take it! You cannot go broke making taking a profit.

16. Begin With The End In Mind

"Begin with the End in Mind means to begin each day, task, or project with a clear vision of your desired direction and destination, and then continue by flexing your proactive muscles to make things happen."
                                        Dr. Stephen r. Covey

You have to know what the game plan is. What is the reason of purchase? What are your long term and short term goals? It is a great idea to sit and interview yourself before making a purchase. List a series of questions that need to be answered with a lot of thought and clarity.

- Will this asset be in my portfolio indefinitely?
- Do I plan on selling in 5, 10, or 15 years?
- How does the mortgage need to be structured if I plan on selling sooner than later?

- Where is the money coming from to purchase the deal?
- What is the payout penalty?
- Are all of the investors on board with your game plan?
- Is this an interest only loan?
- What is the term of the loan?
- What happens if there is a downturn in the economy?

You need to do an in depth analysis of your goals. You will have a much better vision for your goal if you ask yourself these questions.

Also, timing the purchase of the property is important as well. If you plan on holding it forever, it is not as important to buy in a low market. If you plan on selling in a few years then it is key to purchase in a slow market.

Also, if things don't go as planned, you need an exit strategy and still make money. I would also have an exit strategy even if you plan on keeping the property forever.

"People are working harder than ever, but because they lack clarity and vision, they aren't getting very far."

Dr. Stephen r. Covey

17. Negotiate An Amazing Deal

"Most investors are aware that the simplest way to increase your return on investment is to pay less initially. When you prepare your offer, think of innovative ways to structure the transaction to obtain your investment at a desired price or terms."

Eugen Klein

Find out what the sellers' motivation of selling is. Give the seller the price they want and negotiate amazing terms. Or give them the terms they want and get an amazing price.

One of the keys to successful real estate investing is the ability to negotiate an amazing deal. You have got to learn the art of negotiation.

There is almost a different language you must speak when you are negotiating. A great book is Negotiating Rationally by Max H. Bazerman

& Margaret A Neale. A strategy proposed by the authors above;

"If you couch a proposal in terms of your opponents potential gain, you can induce them to assume a positive frame of reference and thus make them more likely to make concessions. You can also emphasize the inherent risk in the negotiation situation for them and contrast that with the opportunity for a sure gain that you have offered."

The way the offer is presented will have a huge impact on how the other party will respond.

18. Real Estate Will Always Appreciate in Value

"In the long run real estate appreciates in value regardless of where the economic cycle is. I have never met someone who has held real estate for 10 or 15 years or more and lost money."

Brett White

Even if you make big mistakes in real estate, the market is forgiving over the long run. Try not to make mistakes and you will make a lot of money very quickly.

19. Who's On Your Advisory Team

"Great things in business are never done by one person. They're done by a team of people."
Steve Jobs

When selling or buying, investment properties or principal residences, it is important to have a team of experts to assist in achieving your goals. Your team should consist of realtors, lawyers, accountants, lenders, financial planners, mortgage brokers, building inspectors and insurance brokers.

All of these professionals have a ton of knowledge and experience. These professionals will be very handy when you are confronted with tough situations. You can't invest in real estate alone, these people will be a vital part of your success. Creating a list of your dream team is very easy. These people want to do business with you. Go look for them and create relationships.

20. Land Is A Monopoly

"it is not only a monopoly but it is by far the greatest of monopolies, it is a perpetual monopoly and it is the mother of all other forms of Monopoly."

Winston Churchill

"Roads are made, streets are made, railway services are improved, electric light turns night into day, electric trams glide swiftly to and from, water is brought from reservoirs a hundred miles off in the mountains - and all the while the landlord sits still. Every one of those improvements is effected by the labour and cost of other people. Many of the most important are effected at the cost of the municipality and of the ratepayers. To not one of those improvements does the land monopolist, as a land monopolist, contribute, and yet by every one of them the value of his land is sensibly enhanced. He renders no service to the community, he contributes *nothing to the general welfare; he contributes nothing even to the process from which his own enrichment is derived."*

There is a lot of power in becoming a landlord. The entire system is setup for the landowner. The tax laws were written by business and landowners. Without owning land, you can not fully exploit the tax system.

Also, the landowner grows rich while he sleeps.

21. Financial Literacy Is Key

"The number one problem in today's generation and economy is the lack of financial literacy."
                                    Alan Greenspan

If you do something that 80% of the population is not willing to do, you will definitely stand out in the crowd. Financial education is very boring and dry. That is probably why many people are not financially literate.

"If a man empties his purse into his head, no man can take it away from him. An investment in Knowledge always pays the best interest."
                                    Benjamin Franklin

Knowledge of financing terms and conditions is paramount in achieving your real estate goals. Success in real estate investing hinges largely on an investor's ability to raise financing from one of the many sources available to them. Resources available to everyone: banks, third party lenders, angel investors, syndicators, family, friends. If you learn to speak the language of big banks you will become very successful.

When I say speak the language of the banks, what I mean to say is; know how to approach the banks when you are looking for financing.

There are is a great video by a man named Dan Pena on youtube. He discusses the topic; how to get the f**king money. The video is titled *"Dan Peña - 50 Billion Dollar Man Dan Pena QLA Financing your Dreams"*

If you are looking to fund your deal, I highly recommend you watch this video. Dan Pena says in the video that the banks are flush with cash, the bank managers don't know what to do with all this money. They are looking for deals to fund. The issue is nobody asks them for large amounts of money. You haven't received any funding because you haven't asked.

Change your perception of getting lending. First, find a great potential investment that checks all the boxes. Then interview banks to get lending. Majority of people think the bank can only interview the lendee. This is not true, if one bank denies you, go to the next.

Keys to getting funded:
1. Practice presenting your deal.
2. Ask for more money than you need.
3. Develop a relationship with the banker.
4. You want a banker who can make a judgement call on whether they can go forward with the transaction.
5. Ask the lender what his/her lending limit is.
6. Ask for the max limit. Ask for more money than you need.
7. Banks are more comfortable lending to someone that has a track record.

8. Partner up with someone that has a track record. This creates an instant track record.
9. Dress like the president.
10. Role play and rehearse before the meeting.

There is no lack of capital in the world to fund your real estate deals.

When you apply for a loan, it is very important to provide the banker with all your documents in a professional package.

Personal Information
- ❏ Proof of current address
- ❏ Employment information
- ❏ SIN
- ❏ Photo ID

Proof Of Employment
- ❏ Recent pay stubs
- ❏ Notice of assessment from the Canada Revenue Agency for the past two years

- ❏ Tax returns for the past 2 years
- ❏ Letter from your job stating the length of time you've been with the job

Proof of Financial Stability
- ❏ Financial bank statements from chequing account
- ❏ Financial bank statements from investment or savings accounts
- ❏ Proof of down deposit

Information about your Financial Obligations
- ❏ Credit History

Furthermore, if you plan on becoming wealthy, and I believe you will, then I encourage you to buy some books on personal financial planning. These will pay major interest later on in life.

22. Buy Real Estate Now

"Don't wait to buy real estate buy real estate and wait."

Robert G. Allen

The best time to buy real estate was 10 years ago, the second best time is right now. While you wait for your investment to appreciate, your mortgage will be paid off by your tenants. Then you repeat.

23. Rezone Your Property & Increase the Value

"Big profits in real estate come from changing the legal use of the land"
                                        Mandeep Bhalla

When you purchase a piece of property with the goal of changing the use of the land, you are investing in the profitability of the development. You are not just hoping for a price increase. Hoping for a price appreciation takes a long time and is actually considered to be gambling by some investors.

By changing the legal use of the property you can increase the value of the land. For example, a piece of property that allows for a single family home is usually worth less than land where you can build commercial buildings. A property allowing subdivision or land allowing multi families to be built is worth considerable amounts of money.

Without changing anything other than the usage, you have increased the value. Rezoning properties comes with a lot of work and the rezoning is not always guaranteed. Get in touch with the appropriate experts to do this.

24. Don't Do This

"Don't procrastinate, don't overextend yourself with debt, and don't forget the long-term goal."
Ralph Case

The main reason people won't do anything is because they procrastinate and find reasons not to take action. Write you goal down. Take action every day and keep your eye on the prize.

Debt is a great tool to increase your net worth if used wisely.

On the other hand, do not over extend yourself. There are countless stories of real estate entrepreneurs who fell victim to the merciless real estate market and lost it all.

Take some time to understand how to market moves.

25. Buy Low, Sell High

"It is ironic that when real estate prices are at their lowest point in the cycle the general population becomes fearful of investing."
— *John Murphy*

Generally speaking, if you go against the herd, you will be making the right move. Conventional wisdom is always incorrect. When the media is broadcasting doom and gloom, everyone is selling their investments. This is usually the trough and worst time to sell. When it seems like the good times can never end, this is the worst time to buy real estate. This is usually the top of the market. First, you have to understand that there is a cycle in real estate, then you must learn to identify where you are in the cycle. Then you can take advantage of the deal.

26. Use Leverage Wisely

"Leverage is a double-edged sword that can magnify the losses on a bad investment just as easily as positive returns on a good investment."

John Murphy

Many people have drowned in debt because they were unable to pay their loans back. Positive returns are not guaranteed, the repayment of your loans is a sure thing. Create exit strategies so you are not in a position where you are unable to repay your debt.

Use the 1% rule that was mentioned previously in the book. You should never be putting money into an investment on a monthly basis. The whole point of the real estate investment is for it to pay you on the first of the month.

With leverage you can control a lot of real estate. With a small percentage down payment you have the ability to control the entire property. This is not true for wall street investing.

27. Strategise

> *"Map out your investment strategy, it cost three times as much to fix something later than it does to plan for all eventualities at the start."*
> *Rick Ledding*

There are a lot of investors who make sure that their business can endure the worst case scenario. Your business plan should consist of; who is involved, what is the risk, what is the reward, and what is the context.

Investors should have a very clear strategy before acquiring investments. Does this mean that the strategy cannot be changed to meet your changing goals? No. That is actually one of the benefits of investing in real estate. There are so many different ways of getting rich with this asset class.

You are the CEO of you real estate investing company. The CEO's main responsibility is to strategise and guide the company.

"It's obvious through my correspondence with CEO's that a good leader always offers a clear vision for his or her organization that is both attainable and inspiring."

Douglas Barry

28. Lenders Know Best

"Lenders look for a cushion between what's owed on the property and what's earned from it. Lenders have a way of crunching numbers to determine not only if a building will generate enough income to cover its operating expenses and debt service, but also if the owner will make a profit from the venture. I'd say the lenders have your best interest in mind. "
Gregory D. Warr

Lenders want to make sure that your investment is going to make you money. If the lender is not approving the deal, run the other way. Instead, what investors do is they look for third party lending to make the deal work and at a higher rate than what the bank would lend at. Huge mistake. The investor is destined to fail. Or they will never make enough cash flow to build a massive portfolio. A small mistake like this in the beginning can set you back years.

Create relationships in the banking industry. Learn how to pitch to banks. Banks want to lend money, they have so much money they don't know what to do with it! Give the banks the info they want, so you can fund your deals. Once you create a relationship, you can become a preferred client which is followed by amazing rates and terms.

29. A Taxing Issue

"In this world, nothing can be said to be certain, except death and taxes."
                              Benjamin Franklin

One of the biggest expenses your business will have is tax. As a real estate investor you have to take advantage of all the tax credits and deductions. You must hire a tax expert. There is a difference between a regular accountant and a CPA. The CPA will have much more knowledge on how to save big. The government makes it worthwhile to be a landlord. There are numerous tax advantages of owning real estate.

Some of the tax deductions you can use as a landlord are:

- Interest Expense
- Motor Vehicle Expense
- Insurance Expense

- Management Fees
- Professional Fees
- Home Office expenses
- Property tax deductions

There are many more deductions that can be used to reduce your tax bill. Tax laws are different in every country so make sure you speak to an expert in your area.

Other benefits of owning real estate are:

- There is no tax on appreciation. If you continue to hold your property, you do not pay any transaction fees, taxes, or commissions.
- If you decide to sell, take advantage of the 1031 exchange(in the U.S.). A properly structured 1031 exchange will allow an investor to sell a property, reinvest the proceeds in a new property and to defer all capital gain taxes.

- You can pull capital from your investment by refinancing. This is a non-taxable event.
- Capital Gains are always taxed at a lower rate than regular income.

Even though you can hire a tax expert, I would educate myself on the topic of taxes. You are going to be paying taxes for the rest of your life. It will be of great benefit to you to learn about them.

30. Cash Flow Is King

"If the property doesn't cash flow don't buy it."
Peter Meribian & Astrid Gottfried

If the property does not cash flow, don't buy it. This is possibly one of the most important rules of real estate investing. Make sure you read the financial documents of a potential investment before purchasing. Get your accountant to read the financial statements as well. If you don't have a relationship with an accountant then: First you need to create a relationship. Second, take that accountant out for lunch and have them read the financials. Third, grab a book on reading financials. If you want to be a successful investor, you definitely need to learn how to read and analyze financials.

Ask for the tax returns going back three or more years. A lot of times, sellers will maximize revenue and minimize expenses.

With experience, you will be able to easily identify when numbers are being fudged.

A property that is not cash flowing means that you will be digging into your pockets to pay for; property tax, repairs and much more. The goal is to have real estate pay you, not pay your real estate investment. This is exactly why your home is NOT an investment. Because it does not pay you.

Whenever there is a downturn in the economy, cash flowing properties are the investments that stay afloat.

People that were over leveraged and over extended in terms of how much debt they had, were the ones that were hit the hardest in the downturn of the economy.

If you find a property that cash flows and checks all the boxes, buy it.

31. Protect your real estate investment, screen your tenants

"Ensure that the management company you hire has a good tenant screening process in place and completes periodic site inspections."
                                                                                                         Grant Cardone

When you have a massive real estate portfolio with different classes of real estate, how do you manage everything?

The experienced and successful real estate investor agree on the following; you will have to give up control, you must create a dream team, your team must consist of very competent people.

Also, these people must be professionals at the top of their fields. You will not be able to do it all yourself. A key to success is to hire a management company that spares you the hassles of and not limited to, rent collection, evictions, and maintenance. Also, make sure the manager of your property is being paid well for a good job he/she is doing.

Even the best management companies can get lazy. Check in with your management companies on a regular basis.

One piece of advice I have received many times is to leave a small gift for the tenants the day they take possession of their new place. A small gift goes a long way. At the end of the day, this is relationship between tenant and landlord, if you treat your tenants good, they will treat your property good.

32. When It's Hard To Find A Good Deal As A Buyer It's A Great Time To Sell

"As an investor-entrepreneur, I've always tried to be contrarian, to not go against the crowd, to identify opportunities in places where people are not looking"

Peter Thiel

Everyone has heard of the Vancouver real estate market and what happened recently in 2017 and 2018. There was a frenzy of buyers making ridiculous offers on properties with no regard to the actual value. Sellers were hoarded with multiple offers when they listed their homes for sale. The bidder with the highest price and best terms, which was usually a no condition cash offer, won the property.

These are the characteristics of an amazing market to sell in.

If you happen to find yourself in this kind of market, sell your property because you will most likely be presented with an offer you cannot deny.

33. Never Lose Money

"Buffett's rules: rule number one, never lose money, rule number two, never forget rule number one."

Warren Buffett

Even though he was in a totally different industry, this rule is very applicable. There is too much information in the world on real estate for you to lose money. Real estate investing is definitely easier and less riskier than wall street investing.

I am very confident that if you apply all of the rules in this book, you will not lose money.

Instead you will create a massive portfolio. Live an optionless life. Losing money is not an option.

34. Lucky Or Smart

"The best entrepreneurs can actually learn to create luck."

Bo Peabody

I agree with Bo. I think you can create your own luck in business. The more frogs you kiss, the more likely you are to experience luck or success. Basically what that means is that you are a resourceful person. You do not accept defeat, you continue to work towards your goal until it is accomplished. In real estate, the more you network, grow your skills and abilities, and consistently show up, the luckier you will be. Donald Trump said, "The harder I work, the luckier I get".

Choosing the right vehicle at the right time is a rare and highly profitable skill that can be learned.

Real estate as a vehicle to achieve massive financial goals has been used by many people.

There are not many assets in the world that can be controlled with small down payments. To purchase commercial, cash flowing real estate, you need a down deposit of about 20% to 35%. To purchase a single family home, you can have as low as 5% down. With low down deposits, you are more likely to earn higher returns on your cash.

Example:

A home worth $100,000 requires at least 5% down. 5% down deposit equals $5,000. Your mortgage will be $95,000. With current interest rates, your mortgage payment will be about $500 a month. If you can rent the home for $1,000, you have a cash flow of $500 a month.

If you have $20,000 saved up, you can theoretically control 4 homes.

Always budget for closing costs.

This is the foundation of all successful real estate investing. This is a very simple example, but you can scale this up to much larger properties. The concept is the same. You will become a very lucky person as soon as you have some mailbox money arriving at the first of every month. Not only will you feel lucky, you will also live longer. People that have generated passive income live longer and healthier and happier lives.

35. Keep An Eye On Your Investments

"Make sure you are aware of what is happening to your property on a regular basis."
Peter Meribian & Astrid Gottfried

Even if you have a management company, you still have to make sure that your investment is operating efficiently as possible.

Hire a well known management company that already has a big portfolio. Do reference checks and interview multiple companies.

If you plan on buying a mutli-family, adding value and eventually flipping it for a profit, then you will have to work in tandem with the management company to make necessary changes.

For example, if you want to renovate each unit, the management company can be at the forefront of the renovation because you will not have contacts of reputable contractors in every market. You will have to work closely with the management to approve all of the changes that will be made.

Many people assume that once you purchase the asset, you can now leave it alone to earn you money. The truth is actually that once the property has been purchased, this is when the real work begins. Real estate investing is not a passive job.

If you want to add value to your deals, if you want your assets to be looked after the way you would, then you will have to communicate regularly with the management company. You have to give them attention, in a way they are your children.

36. Never Stop Learning

"Attend seminars, Ask Questions. Seek Information. Help Others."
George Vernon

Always invest in yourself. Although market knowledge is needed to be successful, if you cannot apply and execute the knowledge, it is worth absolutely nothing. There is no power in having information hog up room in your brain.

Mark Cuban recently spoke about one of the traits that he sees in all billionaires around the world; high learnability. You must have a voracious appetite for new information. It is not a coincidence that Buffet, Gates, Cuban and many many others read for hours a day. They also happen to be the richest people in the world

"Just continuously learn, because particularly in the tech industry, the only constant is change," Cuban explains. "So you've got to stay up, because otherwise, there is some 12- or 18-year-old kid that is coming in with a better idea to kick your a--."

Mark Cuban

The more your learn, the more your earn. There is a direct correlation between how much you read and the amount of money you make.

37. Disclose

"When you are selling real estate three important rules are disclose, disclose, disclose!"
                                               David Mossler

Better to disclose than to be sued. Especially if you know there is a latent defect with the property. A latent defect is a defect that is not discoverable by reasonable or customary inspection. Many, many sellers have been sued because they did not think it was important to disclose a material latent defect. This is not a good idea, you may or may not lose the buyer by disclosing the defect, but at least you will not be sued for large sums of money after you sell your property.

38. Location, Location, Location

"Neighborhoods that are 10 to 35 years old represent areas where the average middle class citizen lives."

Steve Berges

There are so many factors when determining a location to invest in. When you are looking for rental properties, one sure way of finding a great neighborhood is to find the sweet spot. The sweet spot, in terms of age of neighborhood is between 10 to 35 years old. Less than 10 years old and the home will be too expensive. A neighborhood that is 35 years or older is usually run down and in c class areas.

Also, look for strong sales history in the area. Ask your realtor what the average days on the market for the area is. Average days on market is a very good indication of whether this area is desired or not.

Be observant of the curb appeal. What does the landscaping of the area look like? Are the lawns mowed? Are there any junk cars in the front yard? Are the newspapers over flowing out of the mailboxes? What type of fence is used in the front yards? Is it a metal fence or cedar fence? If the property has window bars, it is probably not a safe area. People that are proud of where they live, tend to treat their home, whether it is a rental or not, with more care.

You can also go on to government websites that provide information about the community. Bureau of Labor Statistics is an excellent source of demographic information. *https://www.bls.gov/cps/demographics.htm*

Stats Canada is also another website to get information on demographics.

https://www.statcan.gc.ca/eng/start

The reason why the location of the property is so important is because it influences who your tenants will be and it also influences the amount of appreciation of the investment. The environment in which you plan to buy your real estate investment is just as important as the property itself.

I prefer to invest in an area that is growing in middle class family population. Middle class families are the backbone of countries. They are hard working people and make awesome tenants. Furthermore, there is usually less crime in areas with new young families. These factors create an ideal investing environment. Drive around in the area if you can. Invest in an area with great people. Those areas are the ones to appreciate.

39. Construct your own investment

The primary advantage of building your own investment is that you are able to earn a better than average return on your investment. This is of course if you are able to find a piece of property that is for sale at a discounted price. Also the cost of construction plus land has to be less expensive or equivalent to pre existing investment properties.

If you can find underpriced land ,the cost to you will be much lower if you build, instead of finding an investment property for sale. The reason this is true is because if you purchase an investment, the seller of the investment is going to mark up the property and earn a profit. By building your own investment, you can eliminate the markup of purchasing a pre existing investment.

This is not true for all markets and situations. I recommend you only do this if you have had many years of building and investing experience.

1. Select your site

Before you start the design of the building, you need to find and get to know your lot. It is very important to understand the regulations and restrictions that may impact the siting and design of your new building. Your home must be designed and built to respond to the unique requirements of your lot.

2. Financing & Budgeting

Financing the construction of a new home differs from that of buying an existing home. You must establish relationships with many professionals in the field. The budget is created to prioritize your spending.

3. Home Design and approving plans

A design professional or architect will ensure that your new home will meet all the local building codes and requirements. A building permit will be obtained prior to commencing the construction.

4. Construction Completion

Something as complex and expensive as the construction of an investment is best built with a sense of teamwork. The subcontractors and suppliers are active participants in the project and take responsibility for the quality and scheduling of their Work.

This is the process of building an investment property.

40. Create Cash Flow

"Create an endless income stream of income by holding not selling your investment real estate."

George Vernon

Create cash flow, so when you are retired, you don't have to rely on your pension. Pensions do not get the job done. There is no way to guarantee that the government will not spend this money away.

Hold your real estate assets, let tenants pay the mortgage and interest. Purchase more real estate by leveraging the equity you have built up. Make a goal of purchasing 1,5,10 properties a year. By the time you are retiring, you will have a massive portfolio with no worry of income. If you have 20 properties with each one paying you $500 a month. That is $10,000 a month. There is massive power in real estate investing. This is money working for you.

41. NOI, GRM, CAP Rate

"If you don't know your numbers, you don't know your business"

Marcus Lemonis

The numbers below are for the purpose of the example investment scenario.

Purchase price $800,000
Cap Rate 8%
NOI $64,000
Gross Income $120,000
Operating Expenses $56,000

Cap Rate
NOI / Purchase Price = Cap Rate
$64,000 / $800,000 = 8%

A cap rate will help you determine if the property is worth investing in. Majority of the properties I have seen have a cap rate of 6 percent to 12 percent. Anything outside of these numbers should indicate that there is something wrong with the property. Make sure you do you research on the property. Ask for a detailed package of financials on the property.

NOI
Gross Rental Income - Operating Expenses = NOI

$120,000 - $56,000 = $64,000

NOI is short for net operating income. NOI is the number you arrive at after gross revenue is subtracted by your operating expenses. Remember that the debt service still has to be subtracted from the NOI. Debt service is your annual mortgage payments.

GRM
Property Purchase price / Annual Gross Income = Gross Rent Multiplier

$120,000 / $800,000 = 6.667$

You want the GRM to be below 10. The higher the number the less likely the property is to cash flow. In this case the GRM is 6.667. I would definitely purchase this property.

Saying that you should understand the numbers is a huge understatement. Before purchasing your first deal, you should shop at least 100 to 1000 deals on paper. The best and quickest way to see if a deal is even worth investigating further is to analyze the deal against these financial calculations.

42. Risk and Reward

"To thrive as a real estate investor, it is essential to keep your risk level tolerable."
                              Eppich and King

The amount of risk you can handle is very subjective. I think you should always take big risks. Go big or go home. I do not believe in plan B's. Create a vision, plan and execute.

What are the risks that can lead to failure in real estate investing?
Unfortunately, real investing is heavily affected by external factors. Some of those factors include:

1. Cycles
The real estate cycle is a prominent cycle of booms and eventual crashes. If you are unaware of what has happened in previous cycles, you can be in danger of losing a lot of money.

2. Interest Rates

When interest rates rise the market can become very slow. High interest lead to people being unable to get qualified for mortgages. Soon many people are not able to afford homes. Also, this is a time when many people are unable to pay their mortgage payments. You will see a lot of homes being foreclosed on at this time.

3. Political Environment

Political views and government policies play an important role in whether real estate will appreciate. If some of the tax benefits of holding real estate properties are taken away, or if the tax rate at which real estate income is increased, this will adversely affect your real estate portfolio.

Factors that are in your control.

1. Direction

Operations and direction of the business. You have to plan continuously. Remember that execution and hard work trumps everything.

2. Knowledge

The amount of knowledge you have pertaining to investing. Are you an avid reader? You are essentially a CEO of your real estate investing business. The average CEO reads more than 50 books a year. Warren Buffett reads 8 hours a day. Luckily for us, we can access information from the device in the palm of our hands.

3. Tracking Profits and Expenses

Tracking profits and expenses. Many businesses fail because they are not even able to calculate profitability on an investing opportunity. There is a lot of software and apps that can help in this situation. Also, speak to your accountant. Show the accountant the opportunity. They will have a clearer picture of the investment after reading the financials.

4. Can you Persevere?

Your personality. Are you a resourceful person? Are you a resilient person who doesn't easily quit?

5. Location

Do not purchase a
home in a bad area. Spend a lot of time doing research on the area.

The best way to mitigate risk is by focusing on what you can control. There are many factors that can be controlled. ThE factors which you can control will increase your chances of succeeding. You should also be aware of what is going on in the economy. Do not be ignorant to the facts.

43. The 3 Kings

"A property needs to provide you with three returns, equity growth through appreciation, principal reduction, and most importantly, immediate monthly return through cash flow to ride out any market."
— Peter Meribian & Astrid Gottfried

If you have cash flow, you most likely you can ride out any market. Even if property values are decreasing quickly, you will still have cash flow to pay your mortgage. Create a goal to maximize positive cash flow from every property.

Furthermore, the tenants are paying down your mortgage for you. This means every month your equity in the property grows.

Finally, the appreciation of the property becomes a bonus. If you do decide to sell your investment, it is very likely that your property has substantially appreciated over the years.

44. Don't Over Renovate

"Never over renovate; often a fresh coat of paint and good scrubbing will suffice."
　　　　　　Peter Meribian & Astrid Gottfried

Over renovating is a rookie move. When you spend too much money on the renovation, it is hard to get that money back. Cleaning the property in most cases will make a huge impact.

If you are planning on renovating, make a good budget and then estimate how much the rental income can be increased. Can the money spent on the renovation be recouped.

Beginner renovators tend to over renovate. They also don't budget for unexpected costs.

The goal of investing is to maximize the return on investment and cash on cash return. If you are spending money on unnecessary renovations then your return on investment is going down. This is applies for rental buildings.

You can also renovate and flip the property as well. I am currently in the process of renovating and flipping a home in Vancouver.

There are not very many people that want to renovate and flip homes in Vancouver. There are many reasons for this. There is a large amount of money required for down deposits. For an average house in Vancouver, you need about $400,000 for a down deposit and property taxes.

Another reason is because banks do not have mortgages where they will give you money for the house and the renovation. So in excess of the down deposit you must have cash to renovate the home.

If you run your numbers and know the market in which you are investing, you will always come across a great deal. We acquired the home in Vancouver for a below fair market price. We were even outbid by 2 other parties, but those parties were unable to attain financing. Eventually we got the deal. We did our due diligence and removed the subjects.

We were confident in getting this deal because;

We were confident in the after renovation value. The numbers made sense, and there was a healthy profit margin to be made. Lastly and most importantly there were sold comparables that supported a price range in which we wanted to sell the home after it has been renovated.

We will not be over renovating this home. We will be bringing the home up to standard of what we can sell it for. The last thing you would want to do is over renovate. Do not go above the budget and then list the home for a price much higher than what it can sell for. I see this happen so often and it makes me cringe every time. If you just do a little research in the beginning, you will definitely be better off.

Benjamin Franklin said if he had 4 hours to chop down a tree, he would spend 3 hours sharpening his axe. And only 1 hour to chop the tree down. Whether you are dealing with big or small purchase, you got to know your stuff. Sharpen your skills and slay your goals.

45. Numbers Never Lie

"If income is your number one priority, leave your emotions at home and focus on revenue first."
                                     Michael Wintemute

If income is not your number one priority that is a problem of its own. The top line is always revenue, and is the top line for a reason. There is no point in having a business if revenue is not the center of all actions.

We always here business executives talk about the bottom line. The bottom line is irrelevant if 80% of your actions are not focused towards revenue generation. The rest of the financials do not exist without revenue. There is no balance sheet and income statement without revenue. Floyd Mayweather said it best *"Money is not everything, it is the only thing."*

46. Create a Rainy Day Fund

"Always have some cash reserves, you will need them. Buy real estate in different geographical, socio-economic, climatic areas. Some areas will experience downturns and others will enjoy growth. By diversifying your investments you have a better chance of success and balancing your income stream."

George Vernon

There will always be problems, and usually problems in real estate equate to money being spent. Some markets will go up and some will go down. When you have a portfolio that consists of different real estate classes and in different areas, you are hedging your risk.

Take some of the money that you have and create a rainy day fund. That doesn't necessarily mean that you put your money in a safe. It can mean to create another income stream from a different business. Don't put all your eggs into one business.

47. Don't Chase the Market

"As a buyer, don't chase the market, markets are cyclical, if you miss it on the way up, chances are you'll catch it on the way down."
Clara Hartree

This is very true. However, in real estate, the cycles are very long. The market comes down on the elevator and goes up on the stairs. Wait to buy after the market crashes and effortlessly watch your investment appreciate in value.

"Look at market fluctuations as your friend rather than your enemy; profit from folly rather than participate in it."
Warren Buffet

There are alot of investors that wait along time for real estate to go on sale. When real estate does go on sale, which is also known as a recession or depression, these investors go on a shopping spree.

48. Find a Mentor

"Show me your friends and I'll show you your future."

Dan Pena

The people you rub shoulders with, is who you will become. It is so important to find a mentor. If you want to have a real estate investment portfolio that is worth hundreds of millions of dollars, then you need to find someone that has done it. A mentor basically offers knowledge, wisdom and advice.

You can end up wasting a lot of time researching and making mistakes if you don't have guidance. You can save so much of your time by asking your mentor questions that only an expert would be able to answer. We have so many resources now to get in touch with people in any part of the world.

People love to mentor because they want to pay it forward. If you have a mentor, it is likely that you will be asked to be someone's mentor when you are successful as well.

A great analogy for not having a mentor: Imagine landing in a new city, you need to find your hotel and check in. All you have is the address. You decide you don't need any help with getting to your destination. Would you drive around aimlessly? This approach would be time consuming and frustrating.

Or you can use your GPS. The mentor is your GPS, imagine how much faster you can achieve your goals when you have a mentor. Do not underestimate the power of a mentor or coach. A mentor will be key to the door you want to get through.

A great e-book available online for free:
7 surefire ways to ask someone to be your mentor
Type this into google.

49. Think Big

"Whatever goals you set, you need to be constantly readjusting them so that at no time do you reach your goals before your time is up."

Sam Zell

Sam Zell is the founder and chairman of several companies. His net worth is 5.6 billion dollars. He has invested in and created the majority of his wealth in the real estate world. He took advantage of opportunities all around the world.

His philosophy in life has always been to aim high. His definition of a fool is someone who has reached their limit. You need to readjust and create HUGE goals so you never actually reach them. Sometimes it is not easy to think big. Our whole lives we have been conditioned to think realistically. For the benefit of your business, you need to think big.

A great book that I was lucky to come across and read at a very young age was *"The Magic of Thinking Big" by David Schwatrz.* My biggest takeaway from that book is summarized below.

"Believe Big. The size of your success is determined by the size of your belief. Think little goals and expect little achievements. Think big goals and win big success. Remember this, too! Big ideas and big plans are often easier-certainly no more difficult-than small ideas and small plans."

David Schwartz

Thought precedes action, everything around you was just an idea at one point. Create big goals. Goals to businesses are like air to life.

50. Take Control of Your Future

"An investor is in a small percentage of the population who have the fortitude to invest in and take control of their own successful future."

George Vernon

Everything that has been written in this book is irrelevant if you do not take action. Analysis paralysis is a real thing. Doubt and fear are the true destroyers of dreams. Just dive in, you will make mistakes, but it's better than procrastinating.

You will learn a lot along the way. Find mentors, ride along with them so you can avoid the pitfalls. Then do it yourself. The most detrimental thing you can do is procrastinate and wait. We are lucky that we have all the resources literally at our fingertips to achieve any and all goals we have.

The biggest regret in life is unfulfilled potential. The loss from inaction far outweighs the loss from a mistake.

Remember, the truest test of wisdom is not knowledge, it is action. I could not think of a more appropriate quote to end this book than the following;

"Action cures fear. Indecision and postponement, on the other hand fertilizes fear."

www.ingramcontent.com/pod-product-compliance
Lightning Source LLC
Chambersburg PA
CBHW021832170526
45157CB00007B/2772